by Jeri Cipriano

Table of Contents

Introduction 2

Chapter 1
Symbols of a New Nation 4

Chapter 2
Statues, Monuments, and Memorials 12

Chapter 3
Famous Buildings in Washington, D.C. 20

Conclusion 22

Glossary 23

Index 24

Introduction

Have you ever wondered why our flag is red, white, and blue? Or why the bald eagle is our national bird? Our flag and the bald eagle are two **symbols** (SIM-buhls). They stand for our country. Americans come from different backgrounds. The symbols of our country bring us together. In this book, you will learn about these national symbols.

United States flag

Chapter One will tell you about symbols of our country as a new nation. Chapter Two is about a special statue and some monuments and memorials that make people think of the United States. In Chapter Three, you will visit Washington, D.C., our nation's capital. Buildings in Washington are symbols of our history. All the symbols you will read about make us proud to be Americans.

▲ the White House

the bald eagle

CHAPTER 1

Symbols of a New Nation

The Liberty Bell

Ring. Ring. Clang. Clang. The Liberty Bell first rang in the year 1776. It rang on July 8, 1776, to announce the Declaration of Independence. On that day the people in the thirteen colonies said they were free.

The Liberty Bell was rung every Fourth of July to celebrate our country's independence. Then in 1846, a thin crack appeared. The bell was repaired, but it cracked again. Today, the Liberty Bell does not ring. It hangs in Philadelphia, Pennsylvania. But the Liberty Bell is still a strong symbol of freedom and independence.

Primary Source

Thomas Jefferson wrote the Declaration of Independence in seventeen days! This famous painting from the past shows Jefferson and others signing the Declaration of Independence.

◀ the Liberty Bell

CHAPTER 1

The United States Flag

When the United States was new, Americans wanted their country to have its own flag. The flag would be a symbol of freedom.

The first official United States flag was made in 1777. It had seven red stripes and six white stripes. The thirteen stripes stood for the first thirteen colonies. The flag had thirteen white stars sewn on a blue background. Each time a new state joined the United States, a new star was added to the flag. Today, the United States flag has fifty stars.

Have you ever wondered why the flag is red, white, and blue? The thirteen colonies wanted to start a new country. The white stands for this idea. To do this would take courage. The red stands for courage.

U.S. Flag History

**Look at the time line.
It shows how the U.S. flag looked as more states were added.**

1776   1795   1818   1912–1959   1960

SYMBOLS OF A NEW NATION

IT'S A FACT

Some history experts say that Francis Hopkinson designed the first flag. Hopkinson was a signer of the Declaration of Independence. Many people think that Betsy Ross made the first United States flag.

To win freedom from British rule would mean a long battle. The colonists vowed to never give up. The blue stands for the idea of not giving up. Blue also stands for justice, or fairness.

1. Solve This

Today, there are fifty stars on the flag, one for each of our fifty states. What if a new state joined the United States? Arrange the stars in a new pattern that displays fifty-one stars.

7

CHAPTER 1

The flag flies twenty-four hours a day over many buildings. It always flies over the White House and the Washington Monument.

They Made a DIFFERENCE

Mary Young Pickersgill (PIK-er-skill) sewed a very large flag in the summer of 1813. It was thirty feet wide and forty-two feet long. This flag flew over Fort McHenry during the War of 1812. This flag inspired Francis Scott Key. He wrote "The Star-Spangled Banner," which became our national **anthem** (AN-thum).

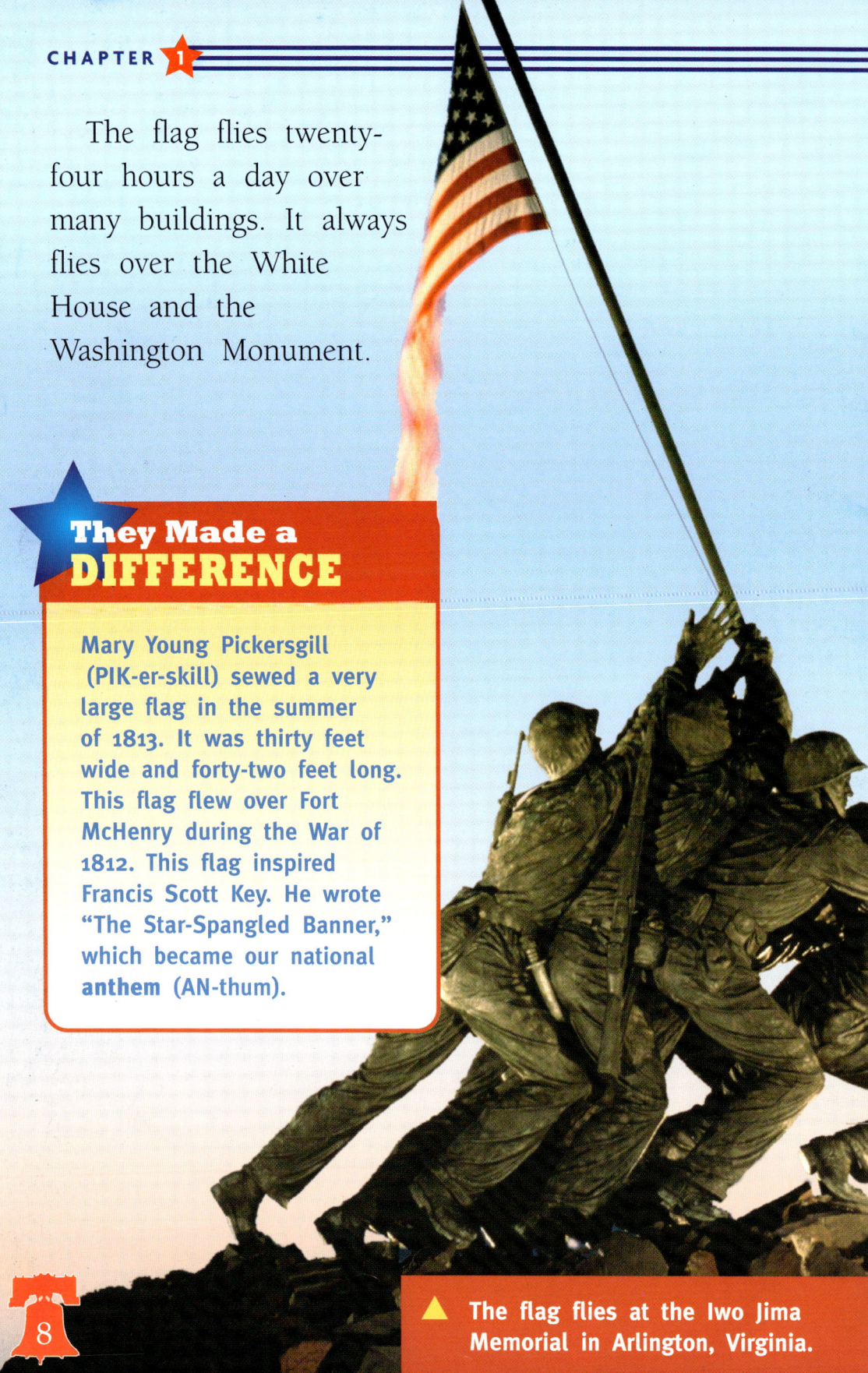

▲ The flag flies at the Iwo Jima Memorial in Arlington, Virginia.

SYMBOLS OF A NEW NATION

The Bald Eagle

When people think of the United States, they often think of the bald eagle. The bald eagle is a symbol of strength, courage, and freedom.

When the United States was a new country, its leaders wanted to choose a national bird. Benjamin Franklin wanted it to be the wild turkey. The wild turkey lived only in the United States and Canada.

Other leaders wanted a bird that looked more powerful. These leaders won. The bald eagle became the official national bird of the United States in 1782.

IT'S A FACT

The bald eagle is not really bald. It just looks that way. Its head is covered with white feathers. The word *bald* comes from the word *piebald* (PIE-bohld). This old word means "marked with white."

CHAPTER 1

The Great Seal

Do you have a dollar bill? Look closely at it. You will see the Great Seal of the United States.

On July 4, 1776, Benjamin Franklin, John Adams, and Thomas Jefferson created a seal for the United States of America. They wanted a symbol to represent the new nation.

The Great Seal was approved on June 20, 1782. It is a symbol of the beliefs of our first leaders.

IT'S A FACT

The opposite side of the Great Seal shows an Egyptian pyramid. The pyramid stands for strength. There are thirteen layers to the pyramid for the thirteen original states. The pyramid is not finished. This shows that the United States will build and grow in the future.

10

SYMBOLS OF A NEW NATION

The "Eagle of **Democracy**" (deh-MOCK-ruh-see) is in the center of the seal. In its beak is a scroll, a rolled piece of paper. The scroll represents the thirteen separate colonies joined to become one nation.

The eagle holds an olive branch in one claw. It holds arrows in its other claw. The olive branch and arrows stand for the power of peace and war.

Look above the eagle's head. Do you see a constellation (con-STA-la-shun), or group, of stars? This stands for the new United States joining the other nations of the world.

CHAPTER 2

Statues, Monuments, and Memorials

Statue of Liberty

The Statue of Liberty is a symbol of freedom to people around the world. The statue was a gift. France gave the statue to the United States in 1884.

The Statue of Liberty is sometimes called "Lady Liberty." The torch in her right hand stands for liberty, or freedom. In her left hand is a stone tablet, or book. The date "July 4, 1776" is written on it. This is the day the United States declared its independence from Great Britain.

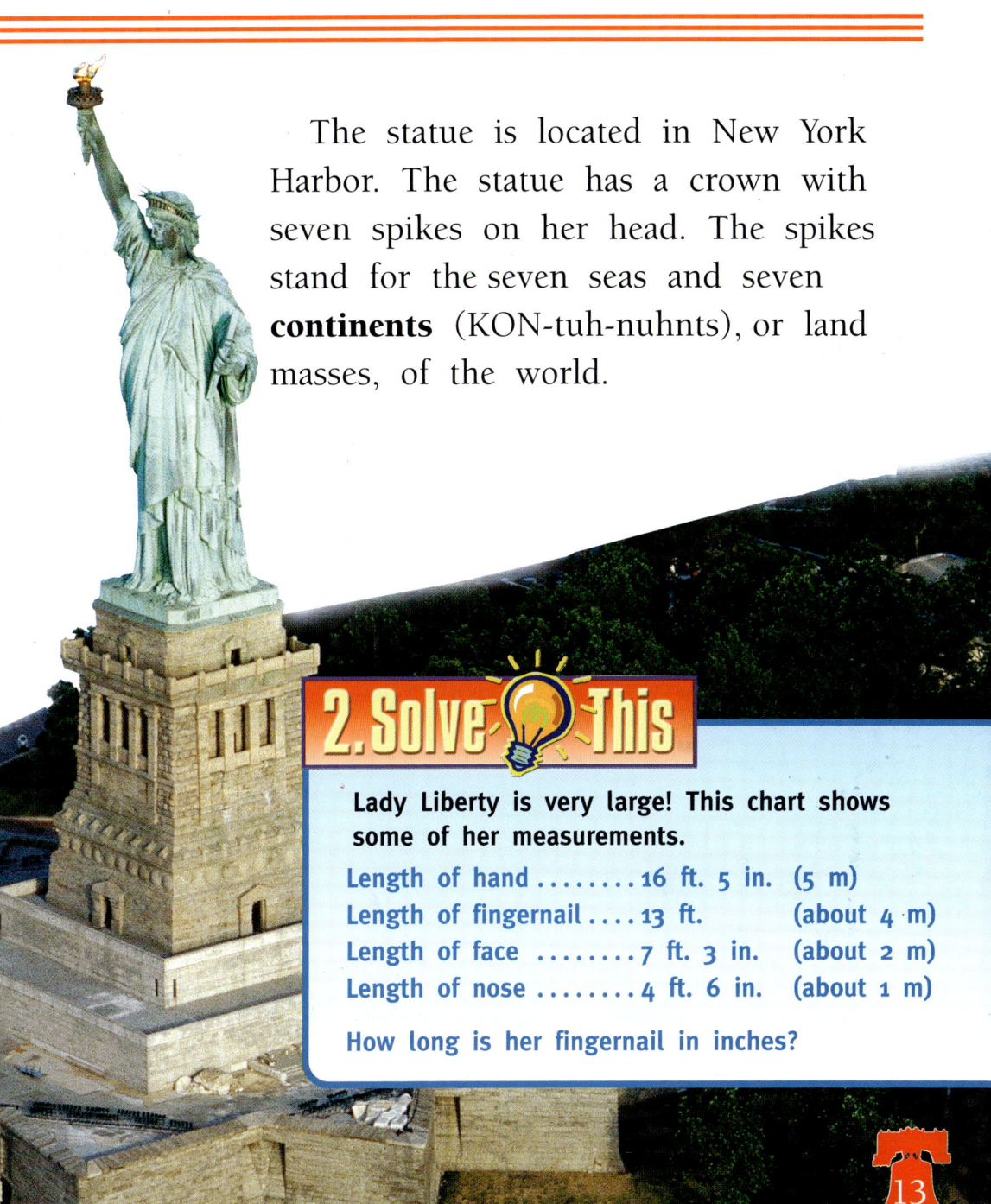

The statue is located in New York Harbor. The statue has a crown with seven spikes on her head. The spikes stand for the seven seas and seven **continents** (KON-tuh-nuhnts), or land masses, of the world.

2. Solve This

Lady Liberty is very large! This chart shows some of her measurements.

Length of hand .... 16 ft. 5 in. (5 m)
Length of fingernail .... 13 ft. (about 4 m)
Length of face .... 7 ft. 3 in. (about 2 m)
Length of nose .... 4 ft. 6 in. (about 1 m)

How long is her fingernail in inches?

CHAPTER 2

Mount Rushmore

It took 400 workers fourteen years to carve the faces on Mount Rushmore. This **monument** (MON-yuh-muhnt) is in the Black Hills of South Dakota.

Mt. Rushmore, South Dakota

Mount Rushmore shows four presidents. They stand for our nation's courage, dreams, freedom, and greatness. George Washington led our new country as its first president.

✓ POINT

Think About It

You have read about several symbols of the United States. Which one do you think best represents the country? Why?

STATUES, MONUMENTS, AND MEMORIALS

Thomas Jefferson wrote the Declaration of Independence. Abraham Lincoln was president during the Civil War (1861–1865). Lincoln declared that all people in our nation are free and equal. Theodore Roosevelt helped the United States become a world power.

IT'S A FACT

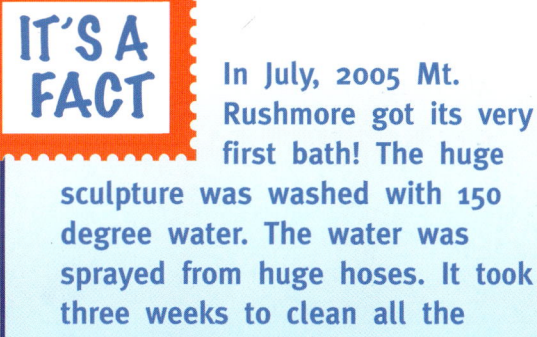

In July, 2005 Mt. Rushmore got its very first bath! The huge sculpture was washed with 150 degree water. The water was sprayed from huge hoses. It took three weeks to clean all the faces. Fifteen men hung in long harnesses to do the job.

CHAPTER 2

Washington Monument

The Washington Monument is the tallest monument in Washington, D.C.. It is 555 feet 5 1/8 inches high (169.29 meters).

STATUES, MONUMENTS, AND MEMORIALS

The Lincoln Memorial

Abraham Lincoln was president during the Civil War (1861–1865). The Lincoln **Memorial** (muh-MOR-e-uhl) is in Washington, D.C. It is a symbol that all people should be free.

A statue of Lincoln sits inside the Lincoln Memorial. It is a building that represents a united country.

CHAPTER 2

Vietnam Veterans Memorial

There is one memorial in Washington, D.C. that gets more visitors a year than any other. It is the Vietnam Veterans Memorial. It honors the brave people who served their country by fighting in a long war. The war was in Vietnam.

The Vietnam Veterans Memorial was built with money donated, or given, by citizens. There was a contest to see who would design the memorial.

They Made a DIFFERENCE

A college student named Maya Ying Lin won the contest to design the Vietnam Veterans Memorial. The memorial is very simple. It is a black, shiny wall. The wall is 500 feet long and more than 10 feet high. The names of people who died in the Vietnam War appear on the wall.

STATUES, MONUMENTS, AND MEMORIALS

CHAPTER 3

Famous Buildings in Washington, D.C.

The White House

The White House address is 1600 Pennsylvania Avenue in Washington, D.C. Every president of the United States except George Washington has lived at the White House. The White House is not just where the president lives and works. It is also a symbol of our country.

▲ the White House

The United States Capitol

The U.S. Capitol is the home of the **Congress** (KON-gris) of the United States. Congress is made up of the House of Representatives and the Senate. They make our country's laws.

The Capitol building has a large dome, or roof. On top of the dome is a statue of a woman. The woman represents freedom.

▼ the Capitol Building

✓ POINT
Make Connections
What does freedom mean to you?

Conclusion

Here are some of the symbols of the United States. What other symbols did you read about?

Glossary

anthem (AN-thuhm) a country's official song (page 8)

Congress (KONG-gris) a branch of the United States government that makes laws; Congress is made up of the Senate and the House of Representatives (page 21)

continent (KON-tuh-nuhnts) one of the seven land masses of Earth: Africa, Antarctica, Asia, Australia, Europe, North America, and South America (page 13)

democracy (deh-MOCK-ruh-see) government that is set up and run by the people who live under it (page 11)

memorial (muh-MOR-e-uhl) something that serves as a remembrance of a person or event (page 17)

monument (MON-yuh-muhnt) a building, statue, or structure that remembers a person, event, or time (page 14)

symbol (SIM-buhl) an object that stands for something else (page 2)

Solve This Answers

1. Page 7 Answers will vary.
2. Page 13 156 inches. 13 feet x 12 inches per foot = 156 inches.

Index

Adams, John, 10

anthem, 8

bald eagle, 2–3, 9

Declaration of Independence, 4, 7

flag, 2, 6–8

Fourth of July, 4

Franklin, Benjamin, 9–10

Great Seal, 10–11

Hopkinson, Francis, 7

Jefferson, Thomas, 4, 10, 15

Lazarus, Emma, 12

Liberty Bell, 4–5

Lin, Maya Ying, 18

Lincoln, Abraham, 15, 17

Lincoln Memorial, 17

Mount Rushmore, 14–15

Pickersgill, Mary Young, 8

Roosevelt, Theodore, 15

Ross, Betsy, 7

Statue of Liberty, 12–13

U.S. Capitol, 21

Vietnam Veterans Memorial, 18

Washington, D.C., 3, 16–18, 20

Washington, George, 14, 20

Washington Monument, 8, 16

White House, 3, 8, 20